Animal Talk

Mexican Folk Art Animal Sounds in English and Spanish

Cynthia Weill
Wood Sculptures from Oaxaca by
Rubí Fuentes and Efraín Broa

Roosters say
COCK-A-DOODLE-DOO
Can you?

Los gallos dicen

KI-KIRI-KI

¿Puedes tú?

What do kitties say?
MEOW MEOW

¿Qué dicen los gatitos?
MIAU MIAU

Fish say
GLUB GLUB

Los peces dicen
GLUB GLUB

Goats say
MEH MEH
Can you?

Las cabras dicen
BEE BEE
¿Puedes tú?

What do tigers say?
GRR GRR!

¿Qué dicen los tigres?

¡GRGRGR GRGRGR!

Cows say
MOO MOO

Las vacas dicen
MU MU

Bees say

BZZZ BZZZ

Can you?

Las abejas dicen
ZUM ZUM
¿Puedes tú?

What do horses say?

NEIGH NEIGH

¿Qué dicen los caballos?
JIII JIII

Dogs say
WOOF WOOF

Los perros dicen
GUAU GUAU

Frogs say
RIBBIT RIBBIT
Can you?

Las ranas dicen

CRUÁ CRUÁ
¿Puedes tú?

What do piggies say?
OINK OINK

¿Qué dicen los puerquitos?

OINC OINC

Lions say
ROAR ROAR!

Los leones dicen
¡RAHR RAHR!

Snakes say

HISS HISS

Can you?

Las serpientes dicen
SSSS SSSS
¿Puedes tú?

Turkeys say
GOBBLE GOBBLE

Los pavos dicen
GORDO GORDO

Owls say

HOO HOO

Can you?

Los búhos dicen

UU UU

¿Puedes tú?

Photo: Jorge Luis Santiago

Rubí Fuentes and Efraín Broa are considered master artisans. Efraín is well known for his elegant figures and Rubí for her delicate and detailed painting. They are members of one of Oaxaca's oldest wood carving families.

Pronunciation Guide

*Cock-a-doodle-doo – Kak-a-du-dul-du
**Ki-kiri-ki – Key-kir-e-key

Moo Moo – Mu mu
Mu mu – Moo moo

Oink oink – Oinc oinc
Oinc onic – Oink oink

Meow meow – Mi-ow mi-ow
Miau miau – Mow-mow

Buzz buzz – Bzzz bzzz
Zum zum – Soom soom

Roar roar – Raaar raaar
Rahr rahr – Raer raer

Glub glub – Glub glub
Glub glub – Glewb glewb

Neigh neigh – Ne ne
Jiii jiii – Heee heee

Hiss hiss – Jis jis
Ssss ssss – Ssss ssss

Meh meh – Me-eee me-eee
Bee bee – Bay bay

Woof woof – Wuf wuf
Gua gua – Gwow gwow

Gobble gobble – Gaab-el gaab-el
Gordo gordo – Gore doh gore doh

Grr Grr – Grr Grr
Grgrgr grgrgr – Grr Grr

Ribbet ribbet – Ribet ribet
Cruá cruá – Crewa crewa

Hoo hoo – Hu hu
Uu uu – Ooo ooo

*pronunciations are best approximation for speakers of Spanish **pronunciations are best approximations for speakers of English

Dedication
To Judith Burton, my dear friend and advisor.

Thanks to

Vicky Weill, Nancy Mygatt, Mollie Welsh Kruger, Ruth Borgman, Myriam Chapman, Stephanie and Fernando Villarreal, Anne Mayagoitia, Sandra Aguilar, Hugo Cerón, J. M. Moracho, Janet Glass, Jan Asikainen, Casa Panchita, Amy Mulvihill, Joyce Grossbard, Susan Milligan, The Field Museum, Rocky Behr, Fernando Pedro, Frank Hebert and The Bank Street Writers Lab

Cover and Book Design by
Sergio A. Gómez

Photography: Otto Piron

FIRST EDITION   10 9 8 7 6 5 4 3 2 1
Library of Congress Cataloging-in-Publication Data Names: Weill, Cynthia, author. Title: Animal talk : Mexican folk art animal sounds in English and Spanish /Cynthia Weill ; with hand-carved animal figures by Oaxaca artists, Rubi Fuentes and Efrain Broa. Other titles: Mexican folk art animal sounds in English and Spanish Description: First Edition. | El Paso, TX : Cinco Puntos Press, 2016. | Series: First concepts in mexican folk art | Parallel English and Spanish texts. Identifiers: LCCN 2015024954 | ISBN 9781941026328 (hardback) ISBN 9781941026335 (e-book) Subjects: LCSH: Animal sounds—Juvenile literature. | Animals in art—Juvenile literature. | Folk art—Mexico—Oaxaca (State)—Juvenile literature. | BISAC: JUVENILE NONFICTION / Concepts / Sounds. | JUVENILE NONFICTION / Animals / Lions, Tigers, Leopards, etc.. | JUVENILE NONFICTION / Art / Sculpture. | JUVENILE NONFICTION / Foreign Language Study / Spanish. Classification: LCC QL765 .W45 2016 | DDC 591.59/4—dc23 LC record available at http://lccn.loc.gov/2015024954